W9-BEQ-963

EXPERIMENTS WITH MOTION

A TRUE BOOK®

by
Salvatore Tocci

Children's Press®
A Division of Scholastic Inc.

New York Toronto London Auckland Sydney
Mexico City New Delhi Hong Kong
Danbury, Connecticut

9/04

This photo is full of motion.

Reading Consultant
Susan Virgilio

Science Consultant
Robert Gardner

*The photo on the cover shows
a tennis ball in motion.
The photo on the title page shows
a spinning top.*

The author and publisher are not responsible for injuries or accidents that occur during or from any experiments. Experiments should be conducted in the presence of or with the help of an adult. Any instructions of the experiments that require the use of sharp, hot, or other unsafe items should be conducted by or with the help of an adult.

Library of Congress Cataloging-in-Publication Data

Tocci, Salvatore.
    Experiments with motion / Salvatore Tocci.
    p. cm. – (A true book)
    Summary: Projects and experiments explore motion and the forces that cause motion, covering such topics as inertia and resistance.
    Includes bibliographical references and index.
    ISBN 0-516-22603-7 (lib. bdg.)   0-516-27467-8 (pbk.)
    1. Motion—Experiments—Juvenile literature. {1. Motion—Experiments. 2. Force and energy—Experiments. 3. Experiments.} I. Title. II. Series.
QC133.5 .T64 2003
531'.11—dc21

2002001593

CHILDREN'S PRESS, AND A TRUE BOOK®, and associated logos are trademarks and or registered trademarks of Grolier Publishing Co., Inc. SCHOLASTIC and associated logos are trademarks and or registered trademarks of Scholastic Inc.
1 2 3 4 5 6 7 8 9 10 R 12 11 10 09 08 07 06 05 04 03

Contents

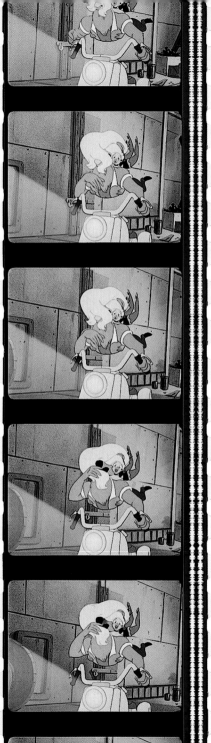

A movie is a series
of pictures that are
projected on a
screen so rapidly
that you think
there is motion.

What's Your Favorite Movie?

Do you know why a movie is also called a motion picture? A movie is simply a series of pictures that are projected on a screen. The pictures are projected so rapidly that you think objects on the screen are in **motion**, or moving.

The history of motion pictures goes back to the 1870s, when two men made a bet. One of the men believed that there were times when a race horse in motion had all four legs off the ground. To win the bet, the man arranged for a photographer to take pictures of horses as they raced around a track. The only cameras available at that time, however, were too slow to take the pictures needed to settle the bet.

A race horse in motion can have all four legs off the ground at the same time.

It took the photographer more than ten years to come up with a way to take pictures of race horses in motion.

The pictures showed that there are times when a race horse does have all four legs off the ground. The photographer became so interested in motion that he started taking pictures of other animals in motion. He even developed a device to project these pictures onto a screen. These were the first motion pictures. People used these pictures to study the motion of animals. All you have to do to study motion is carry out the experiments in this book.

Why Does Something Move?

Saying that something is in motion is another way of saying that it is moving. Some things are easy to get moving. Others are hard to get moving. Still others are almost impossible to get moving. No matter how easy or hard they are to get moving, all these objects have something in common. They all have **inertia**.

Inertia simply means that an object at rest is not going to move unless you do something to it, like push or pull it. This idea was first proposed by an English scientist named Isaac Newton in 1687. His idea became known as Newton's first law of motion. Part of Newton's first law states that an object at rest tends to

Which would you rather get moving— the football or the football player?

remain at rest because of inertia. But do all objects have the same inertia?

Dropping In

You will need:
- tall jar with wide mouth
- table
- scissors
- cardboard
- quarter
- pencil
- paper

Set the jar on the table. Cut a square piece of cardboard a little larger than the mouth of the jar. Place the cardboard over the mouth of the jar. Set the quarter on the cardboard so that it is over the mouth of the jar. Use your finger to flick the cardboard square off the jar quickly. What happens to the quarter?

Place the cardboard on the jar again. Trace the outline of the quarter on the paper. Cut out the circle. This time, set the paper circle on

Be sure to flick
the cardboard so
that it flies
straight off the
jar. You may
need to practice
several times.

the cardboard.
Flick the card-
board off the jar.
What happens to
the paper?

When you first try this experiment, the quarter
and paper probably will fly off the jar and land on
the table or the floor. But with practice, you should

get both of them to fall straight down into the jar. You should have less trouble getting the quarter to do this than the paper. Because the quarter is heavier, it has more inertia than the paper does and is harder to move. So when the cardboard goes flying out from under the quarter, the quarter remains where it is. Without the cardboard to support the quarter, the coin falls straight down into the jar.

The same thing happens to the paper. The paper is lighter and has less inertia than the quarter. Newton's second law of motion states what happens when equal forces are applied to objects with different inertia. If two equal forces are applied to two objects with different inertia, the object with less inertia will move more easily.

The paper has less inertia than the quarter and is therefore more likely to move when you strike the cardboard with the same force. As a result, the paper does not fall straight down into the jar as often as the quarter does.

Experiment with other objects to test their inertia. You can use a button, a piece of candy, a metal washer, or a ring. Are solid objects the only things that have inertia?

Test each object ten times. The one that falls into the jar the most times has the most inertia. Can you rank the objects, starting with the one that has the most inertia?

Staying in Place

You will need:
- measuring cup
- water
- cooking oil
- table
- food coloring

Fill the measuring cup halfway with water. Tilt the cup and carefully pour the cooking oil down the side. Oil and water do not mix. The oil will float on top of the water. Add only enough oil so that it forms a thin layer on top of the water. Set the cup on the table. Place three drops of food coloring on the oil in a straight line.

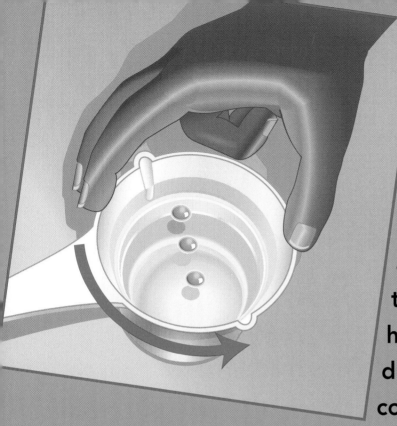

Use your fingers to grasp the cup near the top. Quickly spin the cup about a quarter turn. Watch what happens to the drops of food coloring.

Like solids, liquids have inertia. Because of their inertia, the water, oil, and food coloring do not move even though you spin the cup. It's hard to tell whether the water and oil did not move. But it's easy to follow the drops of food coloring. They stay right where you put them because of inertia. If everything has inertia, then why does anything move?

Experiment 3

Forcing It to Move

You will need:
- empty plastic bottle with narrow neck
- tissue paper
- paper cup
- measuring tape
- transparent tape
- quarter

Remove the top from the bottle. Wet the tissue paper with water. Fold the paper to make a plug that fits tightly into the neck of the bottle. Place the paper cup upside-down over the bottle. Aim the bottle away from your face. Use both hands to squeeze the bottle quickly. Watch what happens to the paper cup. Measure how far the cup moves through the air.

Repeat this experiment, but this time tape the quarter to the bottom of the paper cup. How far does the cup travel this time?

When you squeeze the bottle, you force the air out of it. As the air rushes out of the bottle, it pops the paper plug. The plug then pushes the cup into the air. The force of the air rushing out of the bottle starts the

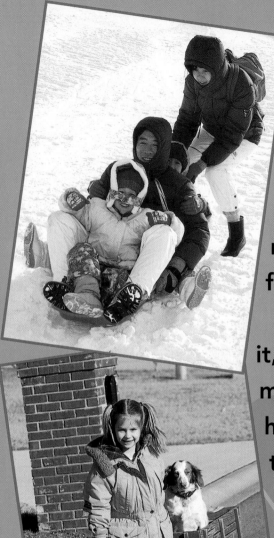

motion of the paper plug and cup. So to set something in motion, you need a **force**. A force is just a push or a pull. In this experiment, motion is caused by a push from the air.

With the quarter taped to it, the cup is heavier and has more inertia. Because the cup has more inertia, the force of the air rushing out of the bottle cannot make the cup travel as far. If you need a force to set something in motion, then how do you stop its motion?

You need a force to get the sled and wagon moving.

Experiment 4

Stopping Its Motion

You will need:
- hard-boiled egg
- large bowl
- raw egg

Place the hard-boiled egg in the bowl. Spin the egg. Grasp the egg gently with your fingers to stop its spinning. Then quickly let go of the egg. What happens? Do the same with the raw egg. Does it do the same thing as the hard-boiled egg?

The push you give both eggs overcomes their inertia and starts their motion. In the case of the hard-boiled egg, both the shell and the egg inside are solids. When you grasp the egg, you force both solids to stop their motion. So you also need a force to stop an object's motion.

The raw egg, however, starts spinning again after you let go. The inside of a raw egg is liquid. When you force the raw egg to stop, all you stop is the motion of the solid shell. The liquid inside is still spinning. The spinning liquid provides the force that makes the raw egg start spinning again after you let go of it.

What Kinds of Motion Are There?

You can see many kinds of motion at a football game. A player running for a touchdown is showing forward motion. A quarterback dropping back to pass the ball is showing backward motion. A football flying through the air is showing spiral motion. There are many other

kinds of motion. For example, one kind of motion occurs when an object swings back and forth. Another kind of motion occurs when an object keeps moving in a circle. Here's a chance to learn something about both these kinds of motion.

Swinging and Spinning

You will need:
- dried peas
- small plastic bucket with handle

Place a handful of dried peas into the bucket. Lift the bucket by its handle and begin swinging it back and forth. Slowly make the bucket swing higher and higher. Keep swinging the bucket so that it starts spinning around in a circle. Do any of the peas spill out of the spinning bucket?

A force keeps the bucket and the peas in motion, spinning around in a circle. This force also keeps the peas from spilling out

25

of the
bucket even when it is upside
down. This force is called a **centrifugal force**.
Try this experiment with water instead of peas.
Centrifugal force should keep the bucket and
water in motion. Centrifugal force should also
keep you from getting wet.

Tilting From Side to Side

You will need:
- ruler
- pencil
- cardboard
- scissors
- string
- LP record

Use the ruler to draw a square with 3-inch (8 centimeter) sides on the cardboard. Cut out the square. Use the pencil to poke a small hole in the middle of the cardboard. Tie a knot in one end of the string. Thread

If you cannot get an LP record, try using a large circle cut out of a glossy piece of cardboard.

the other end through the hole in the cardboard. Then thread the string through the hole in the record.

Hold the record by the string and swing it back and forth. Notice that the record keeps tilting in different directions as it swings. Now grab the record. Hold it level and start it spinning. Start swinging the record as it spins. Does the record tilt this time?

The spinning
motion keeps the record from tilting.
Objects that have a spinning motion resist
any force that acts to change their motion.

What Can a Moving Object Do?

You now know that a force can overcome inertia to set an object in motion. Once an object is in motion, you can make it move faster by increasing the force acting on it. If you keep increasing the force, the object will continue to

The harder you pedal, the more force you apply and the faster you make the bike move.

move faster, or **accelerate**. See what you can do when you make an object in motion accelerate.

Making Sounds

You will need:
- helper
- large lid
- pencil
- thick cardboard
- scissors
- pencil
- ruler
- string
- flexible drinking straw

Use the lid to draw a circle on the cardboard. Cut out the circle. Use the pencil to mark nine points spaced evenly around the edge of the circle. Also mark two points on either side of the center of the circle. Poke a tiny hole through all eleven points with the scissors. Then use the pencil to make each hole larger.

Cut a 3-foot (1-meter) length of string. Thread the string through the two holes near the center. Knot the two ends of the string together to make a loop. Bend the straw and place it in your mouth. Ask someone to stretch out the string by placing a finger from each hand through each end of the loop. Next, ask the person to rotate the cardboard circle to twist the string. Then, have the person let go of the circle and pull the string with both hands as soon as the string begins to twist near his or her fingers. As the

circle spins faster and faster, use the straw to blow air through the holes from one side. What do you hear?

The circle makes a strange noise as it spins faster and faster. The solid cardboard stops the air you blow while the holes let the air pass through to the other side. So the spinning circle breaks up the flow of air. This change in the air flow makes the different sounds. The faster the circle spins, the higher the **pitch** of the sound. What else can an object that moves faster and faster do besides making pitch increase?

Experiment 8

Lifting It Up

You will need:
- scissors
- empty milk carton (quart size)
- string
- ruler
- wooden spool
- small roll of tape like electrical tape
- marbles

Cut the milk carton in half. Keep the bottom half. Use the scissors to poke a tiny hole on either side of the carton near the top. Cut a piece of string that is about 6 inches (15 cm) long. Tie a knot at one end. Thread the free end through the holes and then tie another knot to make a "handle."

Cut another piece of string
that is about 18 inches (46 cm) long. Tie one
end to the handle. Thread the free end through
a wooden spool. Then tie the free end around a
small roll of tape. Hold the spool in one hand.

Start twirling the spool slowly so that the roll of tape starts spinning around in the air. Slowly make the tape spin faster and faster. What happens to the milk carton?

As the tape spins faster and faster, it provides enough force to lift the milk carton and pull it up toward the spool. How much weight can the spinning tape lift? Experiment by placing marbles inside the milk carton. Add one at a time. How many marbles can the spinning tape lift?

You see motion whenever anything moves. A force is needed to set an object in motion. The force overcomes the object's inertia.

A football player must apply a lot of force to stop the forward motion of another player.

While it is in motion, an object can move in many different ways. If the force on the object keeps increasing, then the object will move faster and faster. A force is also needed to slow down or stop an object in motion. Sometimes, the force has to be very powerful to stop a moving object.

Fun With Motion

Newton actually came up with three laws about motion. His third law states that for every action, there is an equal and opposite reaction. Here is a fun experiment to conduct to see an example of Newton's third law of motion.

Experiment 9

Speeding Along

You will need:
- scissors
- measuring tape
- string
- straw
- balloon
- two helpers
- masking tape

Cut a 10-foot (3 m) long piece of string. Slide the string into the straw. Blow up the balloon. Pinch the opening tightly so that no air escapes. Ask your helpers to use two pieces of masking tape to attach the balloon to the straw. Then have your helpers stretch out the string and hold it tightly and level. Move the balloon and straw toward one end of the string. Release the balloon and watch what happens.

Make sure you pull
the string tight
and hold onto the
balloon at the
same time.

The arrows show that the air rushing out is an action that causes a reaction—pushing the balloon forward.

When you release the balloon, the air inside rushes out the open end. The air rushing out is an action in one direction that causes an equal reaction in the opposite direction. Experiment to test Newton's third law of motion. For example, fill the balloon with only half as much air as you did before. The air rushing out this time should produce an action with only half the force. Does the balloon travel only half the distance this time?

To Find Out More

If you would like to learn more about motion, check out these additional resources.

 **Books**

DiSpezio, Michael. **Awesome Experiments in Force & Motion.** Sterling Publishing, 1998.

Gardner, Robert. **Experiments with Motion.** Enslow, 1995.

Gold-Dworkin, Heidi and Robert K. Ullman. **Learn About the Way Things Move.** McGraw-Hill, 2000.

Graham, John. **Forces and Motion.** Larousse Kingfisher Chambers, 2001.

Madgwick, Wendy. **On the Move.** Raintree Steck Vaughn, 1999.

Murphy, Bryan. **Experiment with Movement.** Lerner Publications, 1992.

Science Museum of Minnesota
120 W. Kellogg Boulevard
St. Paul, MN 55102
651-221-9444
http://www.sci.mus.mn.us/ sln/tf/m/motionmachine/ motionmachine.html

Accept the challenge to use materials left over from a holiday season to make a machine that makes at least one motion. This site will show you some that students submitted, including a dog bone delivery car and an egg cracker.

"Rocket Man"
http://www.discovery cube.org/kids/ rocketMan.htm

This site shows you how to build a simple rocket using plastic film containers. When you blast your rocket into the air, you will see another example of Newton's third law of motion.

"Whirling Watcher"
http://www.exploratorium. edu/snacks/whirling_ watcher.html

Learn how to build a stroboscope that will make a moving object seem to jerk along, change speed, or even move backward.

Important Words

accelerate to increase an object's speed

centrifugal force a force on an object that keeps it moving around in a circle

force the push or pull on an object

inertia the force that makes something that is at rest stay still and something that is moving stay in motion

motion movement

pitch a quality that a sound has

Index

Meet the Author

Salvatore Tocci is a science writer who lives in East Hampton, New York, with his wife, Patti. He was a high school biology and chemistry teacher for almost thirty years. As a teacher, he always encouraged his students to perform experiments to learn about science. He loves to accelerate his convertible sports car to overcome inertia and push it to the speed limit.

Photographs © 2003: AP/Wide World Photos/Rob Carr: 7; Dembinsky Photo Assoc.: 20 bottom (Dan Dempster), 24 right (Patti McConville), 2 (Richard Hamilton Smith); Folio, Inc./Jeff Greenberg: 20 top; Fundamental Photos, New York/Richard Megna: 29; Photo Researchers, NY: 38 (Junebug Clark), 31 (Tim Davis); PhotoEdit/David Young-Wolff: 24 left; Photofest: 4; Stock Boston/Bill Bachmann: 11; The Image Bank/Getty Images/Malcolm Piers: 1; The Image Works/James Pickerell: cover.

Illustrations by Patricia Rasch